Trick or Treat

Clarkson Potter
Publishers
New York

By Emily
Gwathmey
and Suzanne
Slesin

Designed by
Alexander Isley
Design

TO OUR FAVORITE TRICK OR TREATERS:
ANNIE, JAKE, AND LUCIE

CONTENTS

Hallowe'en

Treats

Hallowe'en, with its roots in the spooky happenings of the past, has become a wildly popular night to celebrate on a supernatural theme. Donning costumes to go trick or treating, decorating the house with garlands of ghosts or skeletons or stretchy spider webs, carving pumpkins into grinning jack-o'-lanterns —all are required for this special spectral happening.

October 31 was also always believed to be the most propitious night for divining the future. So fortune-telling, with its questions about love and marriage, children, health, and death, was an activity around which many party games revolved. And apples, nuts, cabbages, and cakes were used to come up with the answers.

In Scotland today, an old game is played in which a boy and a girl walk into a kitchen garden, shut their eyes, and each pull up a cabbage. If the stalk is straight, he will marry someone strong and healthy; but if it is shriveled or crooked, his mate will be sickly. If earth clings to the roots of her cab-

bage, she will marry someone rich; if the roots come clean, she will wed a poor man.

Then there is the story that says if a woman looks into a mirror on the stroke of midnight and cuts an apple into nine slices, holding each piece on the point of a knife before she eats it, she may see in the moonlit glass the image of her lover looking over her left shoulder, asking voicelessly for the last bite.

For modern Hallowe'en festivities, Peggy Cullen, a professional baker, has created six original, delicious, and eerily decorative recipes that are meant for both grown-ups and children to enjoy. Now all that's needed is a broom, a couple of rolls of orange and black crepe paper, and some suitably scary masks.

CRUNCHY BONES COOKIES

2 **cups** toasted and ground hazelnuts
1 1/2 **teaspoons** ground anise seed
2 **cups** confectioner's sugar
2 very fresh egg whites, at room temperature

1. Preheat the oven to 350° F.

2. Combine the nuts, anise, and confectioner's sugar in a food processor. Pulse the machine about 15 times to blend and transfer to a medium bowl.

3. Beat the egg whites vigorously with a fork until they are foamy, about 1 minute. Moisten the nut mixture with 4 tablespoons of the whites and mash with a rubber spatula to evenly distribute the liquid. Knead with your hands until the mixture is moist enough to form a ball.

4. Divide the dough evenly into 24 balls and roll each into a rope about 6 inches long; flatten it to about 1/2 inch wide. Score each end with a blunt knife. Place on an ungreased baking sheet about 2 inches apart. Bake for 8 to 10 minutes, until the tops begin to brown lightly. Cool the cookies completely on the sheet before removing. Makes 24 cookies.

8

A skeleton once in Khartoum
Asked a 𝔰𝔭𝔦𝔯𝔦𝔱 *up into his room;*
They spent the whole night
In the eeriest fight
As to which should be frightened of whom.

—*Anonymous*

IN ENGLAND, HALLOWE'EN IS CALLED
"NUTCRACK NIGHT." THAT'S WHEN SWEETHEARTS
THROW NUTS INTO A FIRE. IF THEY
EXPLODE, A BAD MARRIAGE IS IN STORE. IF THEY
BURN QUIETLY, A GOOD MARRIAGE LIES AHEAD.

GRAVEYARD GATEAU

marzipan tombstones

Confectioner's sugar for rolling
3 ¹/₂ ounces marzipan

the devil's cake

2 cups flour
2 teaspoons baking powder
2 teaspoons baking soda
1 teaspoon salt
4 ounces semisweet chocolate,
   coarsely chopped
6 tablespoons plus 1¹/₄ cups unsalted
   butter, softened
2 cups granulated sugar
2 cups water
2 eggs, at room temperature, lightly beaten
1¹/₂ cups confectioner's sugar
¹/₄ cup milk
Green food coloring
1/2 cup plus 1 tablespoon
   unsweetened cocoa

GREETINGS FOR HALLOWEEN

We invite you to meet with
us at...............................St.
at the hour of ....o'clock
to hold revel on the mystic
HALLOWE'EN

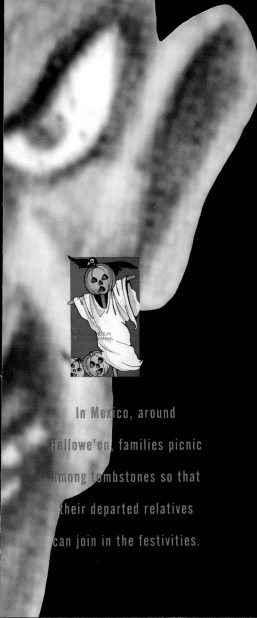

In Mexico, around Hallowe'en, families picnic among tombstones so that their departed relatives can join in the festivities.

1. Make the tombstones at least 3 days ahead so that they can dry. On a surface dusted with confectioner's sugar, roll the marzipan out to a thickness of $1/8$ inch and cut out 7 or 8 gravestones of different shapes and sizes. Leave them on a rack in a warm, dry place for a few days until they are stiff and dry.

2. Preheat the oven to 350° F. Butter and flour a 9 x 13 x 2-inch pan. In a large bowl, sift together the flour, baking powder, baking soda, and salt. In another bowl, combine the chocolate and 6 tablespoons butter. Mix the granulated sugar and water in a small pot and bring to the boil. Pour the hot sugar syrup into the chocolate-butter mixture and stir to melt. Let cool slightly and whisk in the lightly beaten eggs. Add the liquid to the sifted dry ingredients and stir to combine. Pour into the prepared pan and bake until a toothpick inserted in the center comes out clean, about 25 minutes. Allow the cake to cool in the pan for 10 minutes, then turn out onto a rack to cool completely.

3. Beat together the $1^1/4$ cups softened butter and the confectioner's sugar until light and fluffy. Beat in the milk. Remove 2 tablespoons of the icing and color with green food coloring. Beat $1/2$ cup of cocoa into the remaining icing. Frost the sides and top of the cake and sift 1 tablespoon of cocoa over the surface. Insert the tombstones into the cake at crooked angles. Drop green icing from a fork to create little tufts of grass at the base of each tombstone.

FILLET OF A FENNY snake,

IN THE CAULDRON BOIL AND BAKE;

EYE OF NEWT AND TOE OF FROG,

WOOL OF BaT AND TONGUE OF DOG,

ADDER'S FORK AND BLIND-Worm's STING,

LIZARD'S LEG AND HOWLET'S WING,

FOR A CHARM OF POWERFUL TROUBLE,

LIKE A HELL-BROTH BOIL AND BUBBLE.

- WM. SHAKESPEARE

ITCHES' BREW
WITH GHOSTLY MANIFESTATIONS

1 generous cup miniature marshmallows
24 whole cloves
¹/₂ gallon apple cider
3 cups grape juice
¹/₂ cup orange juice
3 tablespoons lemon juice
3 tablespoons star anise (about 48 stars)
1 teaspoon cinnamon
¹/₂ teaspoon nutmeg
1 tablespoon finely sliced fresh ginger

1. Preheat the oven to 250° F. Butter a baking sheet and sift confectioner's sugar over it. Arrange marshmallows into 12 vaguely triangular shapes to form ghosts, about 8 or 9 marshmallows per ghost. Bake until they melt, about 5 minutes. Do not let them brown. Insert 2 cloves for eyes into the top marshmallow of each triangle. Let the ghosts cool completely on the tray before removing them with a spatula.

2. Combine the remaining ingredients in a large pot and place it over medium heat until the mixture is warm to the touch. Do not let it come to a boil. Let the brew stand for at least 2 hours. Transfer to a punch bowl and float the ghosts on top. Serve cold or at room temperature. Makes 3 quarts.

Note: The brew can also be served hot, but the ghosts will soon vanish into the warm liquid. Dark rum or vodka can be added to the brew, or to individual glasses.

OOTHSAYER'S SLICED APPLES

8 ounces semisweet chocolate, coarsely chopped
1/4 cup pecans, finely ground
6 large, firm apples
1/2 cup sugar

1/2 cup heavy cream
1/2 cup dark corn syrup
2 tablespoons unsalted butter
Pinch of salt
1/2 teaspoon vanilla extract

1. Place the chocolate in a double boiler over medium heat until it is almost melted. Remove from heat, stir, and let cool.

2. Spread the nuts in a small bowl.

3. Dip the apples into the chocolate and shake off excess. Then dip the apples into the nuts to coat the bottom. Set them 3 inches apart on a lightly buttered tray and refrigerate for 45 minutes.

4. In a small pot, stir together the sugar, cream, corn syrup, butter, and salt. Cover and bring to a boil over medium heat. Cook until the mixture reaches 240°, stirring occasionally. Remove pot from the heat and add vanilla. Pour the hot caramel over the apples, a little at a time, letting it drip down the sides. Cool the apples but don't refrigerate them.

5. When ready to serve, slice the apples in half and remove the cores. Cut each half into 4 slices. Makes 48 slices.

Seeds of Love

Pick two apple seeds and name them for two different lovers. Place them on the eyelids. The length of time the seeds stay on shows which contender is truer. Blinking can tip the hand of fate.

Who's My Love

I pare this apple round and round again;
My sweetheart's name to flourish on the plain:
I fling the unbroken paring o'er my head,
My sweetheart's letter on the ground to reach.

~Old Postcard

TO CURE JAUNDICE, SWALLOW A LARGE LIVE HOUSE SPIDER, ROLLED UP IN BUTTER.

To cure a fever, wear a spider in a nut shell around the neck.

Halloween

Ducking for Apples

Kindly promote ghostly interests during this season.

SPECTRAL SPIDERS

6 ounces semisweet chocolate, finely chopped
¹/₃ **cup** currants

1. Divide the chocolate evenly between two small heatproof bowls. Warm one bowl of chocolate in a double boiler until halfway melted, then stir to melt completely. Stir in the currants. Melt the second bowl of chocolate in the same way and set aside to cool.

2. On a baking sheet lined with waxed paper, spoon out 18 to 20 little clusters of chocolate currants, about ³/₄ inch in diameter each, placing them about 4 inches apart. These are the spider "bodies."

3. Pour the remaining chocolate into a small ziplock plastic bag. Close the top and snip a tiny piece from a corner to make a "writing" tip. Form the 8 legs by gently squeezing the chocolate from the bag over the "body" of each spider in two opposite X's, extending each leg about 1 inch from the center. Be sure the legs are well joined at the body. Refrigerate for 30 minutes or until the chocolate has completely hardened. Peel the spiders off the waxed paper.

4. If you're using a paper tablecloth, melt about 5 ounces of white chocolate in the same way and "pipe out" a spider web directly onto it, for the spiders to sit on. Makes 18 to 20 spiders.

"Will you walk into my parlor?" said the spider to the fly;
"'Tis the prettiest little parlor that ever you did spy. The way into my parlor is up a winding stair, And I have many curious things to show when you are there." "Oh no, no!" said the little fly, "to ask me is in vain; For who goes up your winding stair can ne'er come down again."

— Mary Howitt

17

ICHABOD CRANE'S
BAKED PUMPKIN MOUSSE

2 **tablespoons** unsalted butter, softened
1 **cup** superfine sugar
4 **eggs**, separated
5 **tablespoons** yellow cornmeal
1 **cup** canned pumpkin puree

1 **teaspoon** cinnamon
1 **teaspoon** ginger
$^1/_2$ **teaspoon** nutmeg
1 **cup** heavy cream
Pinch of salt

1. Preheat the oven to 350° F. Butter a 6-cup ovenproof bowl.

2. In a large bowl, cream together the butter and $^3/_4$ cup sugar. Beat in the yolks, one at a time. Stir in the cornmeal, pumpkin, and spices, then the cream.

3. Beat the egg whites until they are foamy. Add the salt. Continue to beat until soft peaks form. Gradually add the remaining $^1/_4$ cup sugar, a teaspoon at a time, and continue beating until the whites are stiff and glossy but not dry. Fold the whites into the pumpkin mixture and pour the mixture into the buttered bowl.

4. Set the bowl in a larger pan filled with 1 inch of hot water and bake for $1^1/_4$ to $1^1/_2$ hours, or until a knife inserted in the center comes out clean. Serve warm from the bowl, or let it settle on a cooling rack for 30 minutes and then invert the mousse onto a plate. Make a jack-o'-lantern face with currants and serve with unsweetened whipped cream. Serves 8.

No pumpkins are turned into jack-o'-lanterns in Scotland or England. Instead, carved-out turnips or beets are used to scare witches.

WE HAVE PUMPKIN AT MORNING, AND PUMPKIN AT NOON. IF IT WERE NOT FOR PUMPKIN, WE WOULD BE UNDOON. -PILGRIM SONG

HAPPY HALLOWEEN

Halloween

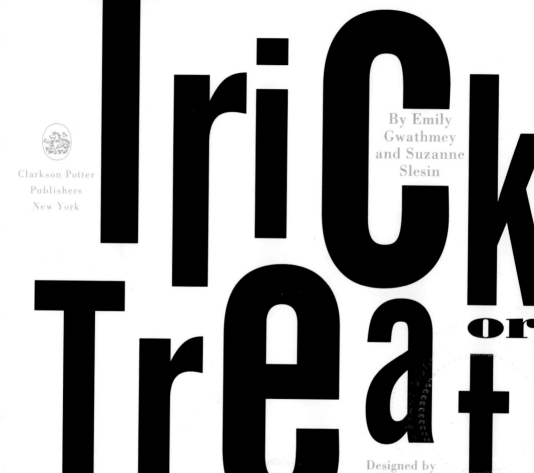

TriCK
TreaT
or

By Emily
Gwathmey
and Suzanne
Slesin

Clarkson Potter
Publishers
New York

Designed by
Alexander Isley
Design

Thank you: Andreas Brown at the Gotham Book Mart
in New York for your generosity and remarkable postcards;
Barbara Hogenson, our agent at the Lucy Kroll Agency;
Roy Finamore, our editor; Howard Klein, our art director;
Alexander Isley, our designer; and Kristen Behrens
at Clarkson Potter.

Published by Clarkson Potter/Publishers, New York, New York.
Member of the Crown Publishing Group.

Random House, Inc. New York, Toronto, London, Sydney, Auckland
www.randomhouse.com

CLARKSON N. POTTER is a trademark and POTTER and colophon
are registered trademarks of Random House, Inc.

Printed in Hong Kong

Library of Congress Cataloging-in-Publication Data
Gwathmey, Emily Margolin.
Trick or treat / by Emily Gwathmey and Suzanne Slesin.
1.Halloween. I. Slesin, Suzanne. II. Title.
GT4965.G93   1992
394.2'683—dc20   91-43014

ISBN 0-517-58887-0

10 9 8 7 6 5 4 3 2

CONTENTS

Tricks

Long Ago, Before it was a night out for children, Hallowe'en was a day out for the dead.

It began during the time of the Celts, who lived hundreds of years before the birth of Christ in what is now France, England, and Ireland. October 31, the end of the Celtic calendar year, was

the day when the crack between the worlds opened and ghosts, witches, goblins, black cats, devils, imps, and demons stalked the earth. Druid priests built giant bonfires to keep them at bay; people hoping to hide from unfriendly spirits dressed in costumes, and they put out sweets to placate demons.

By the ninth century, the Christian church had set aside November 1 as a feast day to honor the saints and called it All Saints' Day or All Hallows. The preceding evening—called All Hallows' Eve, or All Hallows' Even (which was eventually shortened to Hallowe'en)—continued according to pagan beliefs. This was the time when the dead returned to roam the earth, and people danced around fires that lit up the sky and protected them from evil. A celebration followed, with bobbing for apples, nut roasting, and a variety of fortune-telling activities all part of the festivities.

In the mid-1800s, when Irish and Scottish immigration was at its height, Hallowe'en arrived in America. Celebrating this festival offered a connection to the old country. Then, with the turn of the century, Hallowe'en and the Golden Age of Postcards collided. The holiday provided a rich subject for artists and a prime marketing opportunity for publishers. Hundreds of thousands of cards were printed, bought, mailed, and saved. Each cost but a penny or two to buy and a mere penny to send.

Nowadays, there is hardly a place in America that does not honor Hallowe'en. Both adults and children look forward to October 31, when they don costumes, carve pumpkins, and go trick or treating. Because the treats are so forthcoming, the tricks are becoming endangered species. The ancient pagan festival has turned into a quintessentially American night of extravagant fun and frolic. 🎃

To protect against creatures of the night, carry a piece of bread in your pocket.

An ancient Irish legend has it that on Hallowe'en a cave known as the "Hell-Gate of Ireland" opens up and ghosts fly out, wreaking havoc and stealing babies, whom they replace with demon children and changelings.

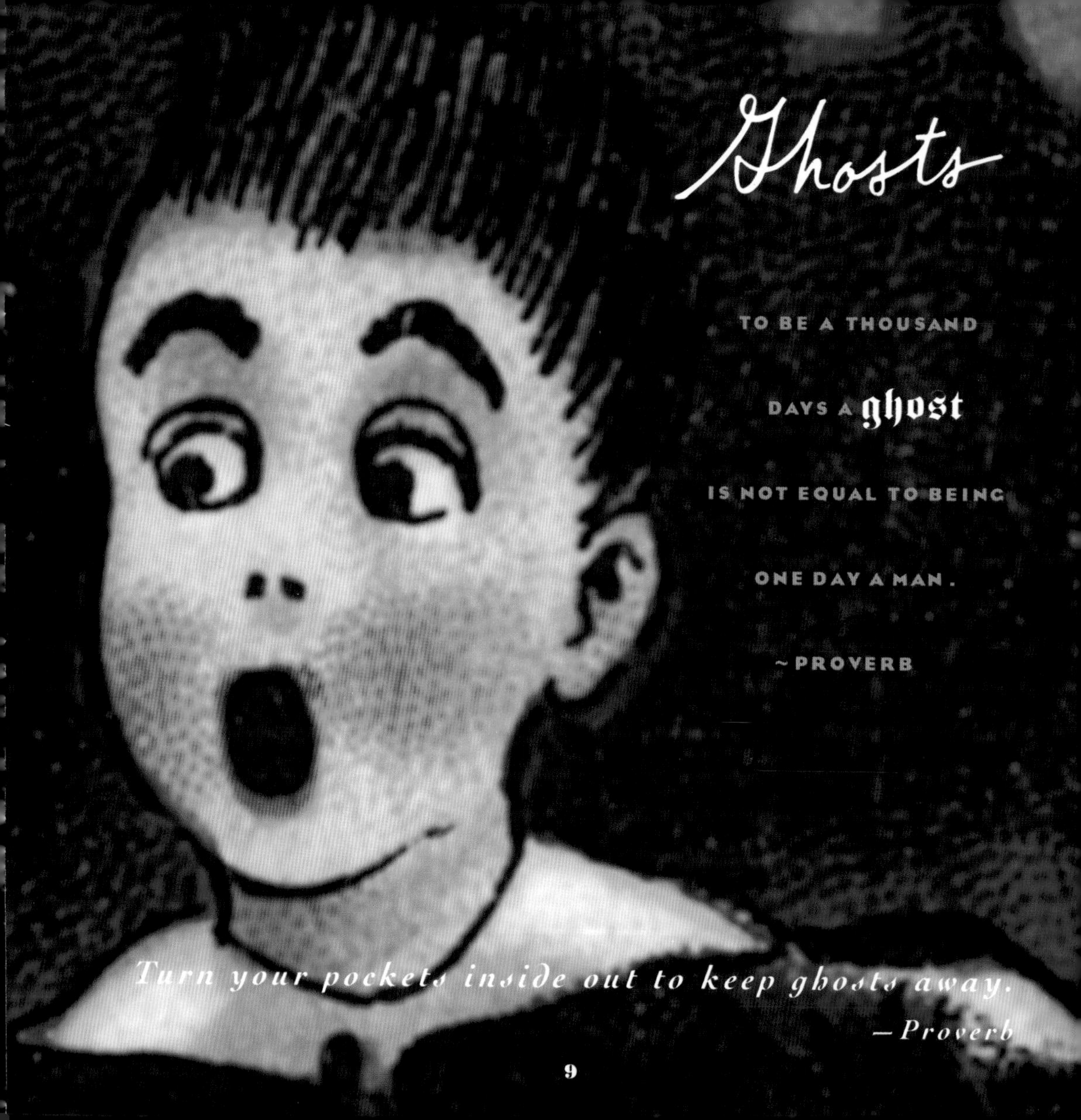

Ghosts

TO BE A THOUSAND

DAYS A **ghost**

IS NOT EQUAL TO BEING

ONE DAY A MAN.

~PROVERB

Turn your pockets inside out to keep ghosts away.

— Proverb

In Celtic lands, on the last day of October,
farmers heaped their tables with food from the harvest
to welcome home their ghosts. Bright flames from
huge bonfires guided kindly spirits on their journeys
back home and frightened evil ones away.

Children born on Hallowe'

Three little ghostesses
Sitting on postesses,
Eating buttered toastesses,
Greasing their fistesses,
Up to their wristesses,
Oh, what beastesses
To make such feastesses!
—Anonymous

en can see and even talk to GHOSTS

THE HAG
    THE HAG IS ASTRIDE
THIS NIGHT FOR A RIDE,
    THE DEVIL AND SHE TOGETHER:
THROUGH THICK AND THROUGH THIN,
    NOW OUT AND NOW IN,
THOUGH NE'ER SO FOUL BE THE WEATHER.
    A THORN OR A BURR
SHE TAKES FOR A SPUR,
    WITH A LASH OF THE BRAMBLES SHE RIDES NOW.
THROUGH BRAKE AND THROUGH BRIERS,
    O'ER DITCHES AND MIRES,
SHE FOLLOWS THE SPIRIT THAT GUIDES NOW.
    —ROBERT HERRICK

A child that has teeth when it is born will grow up to be a

12

Witches

ON HALLOWE'EN IN SCOTLAND, THE DEVIL CALLS ALL WITCHES TOGETHER TO DANCE THE NIGHT AWAY TO MUSIC PLAYED ON A "DEVIL'S BAGPIPE," A MUSICAL INSTRUMENT MADE FROM HENS' HEADS AND CATS' TAILS.

witch *or a* vampire.

If you light a candle at the ends

Twirl it that the air it rends

Should the right end stay lit

All will be gay.

If the left stay lit the witches slay.

If both stay lit you will belt.

If both go out you have routed them out.

—*Old Postcard*

Witches mix herbs such as

deadly nightshade, mandrake,

hemlock, and monkshood

into a magic cream that they spread

over their bodies to propel

themselves, astride their broomsticks,

into the night sky.

This is the nicht o' Hallowe'en
When a' the witchie may be seen;
Some o' them black, some o' them green,
Some o' them like a turkey bean.

~Anonymous

HELL ITSELF BREATHES OUT CONTAGION TO THIS WORLD.

~WM. SHAKESPEARE

For something is amiss or out of place
When mice with wings can wear a human face.
— _Theodore Roethke_

Owls and

If a black cat comes
to meet you, it is good luck.
But if it only comes
halfway, and walks away
from you, it is bad.

The eternal symbol of melancholia, the BAT _sleeps upside down, its_

Avoid grinning black cats, on full green moon,
If your lover is true, he'll come back soon.
It breaks the charm, the witches scream,
And never return, till next Hallowe'en.
~*Old Postcard*

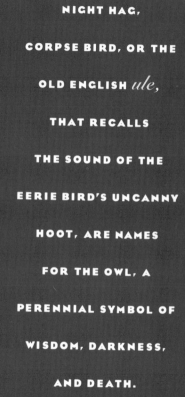

NIGHT HAG,

CORPSE BIRD, OR THE

OLD ENGLISH *ule,*

THAT RECALLS

THE SOUND OF THE

EERIE BIRD'S UNCANNY

HOOT, ARE NAMES

FOR THE OWL, A

PERENNIAL SYMBOL OF

WISDOM, DARKNESS,

AND DEATH.

Bats and Cats

. . . from yonder ivy-mantled tow'r
The moping owl does to the moon complain.

~Thomas Gray

mammoth wings wrapped around itself like *a witch's cloak.*

Telling fortunes, preparing charms, brewing herbal mixtures, and flying about on broomsticks was treacherous, time-consuming work for witches. Owls, bats, and cats were their helpers, or "familiars," and their job was to collect ingredients for spell-casting. The familiars were capable of performing the same magic as the witches. But beware. They might even be the witches in disguise.

AT NIGHT, CATS ACCOMPANIED **witches**

AND BECAUSE OF THE DARKNESS,

ALL WERE THOUGHT TO EMBODY

*Hang a bell of gold
round a cat's
neck at the witching
hour and he'll
do what he's told.
—Old Postcard*

SEEING AN OWL

IN THE DAYTIME IS AN OMEN

OF BAD LUCK.

Old Scratch

The Devil

For Satan finds some mischief still For idle hands to do.
~Isaac Watts

THE DICKENS

Auld Cloots

Belial

𝔅𝔢𝔢𝔩𝔷𝔢𝔟𝔲𝔟

He must have a long spoon that must eat with the devil.

~Wm. Shakespeare

Lucifer

"Halloween"

PRINCE

Halloween Greetings

Speak of the devil and he will hear about it.

MEPHISTOPHELES

Old Horney

Pluto

OF EVIL

An' all us other child-ren, when the supper things is done We set around the kitchen fire an' has the mostest fun A-list'nin' to the witch- tales 'at Annie tells about An' the Gobble- uns 'at gits you Ef you don't watch out!
~James Whitcomb Riley

Masquerade

When I was a little girl,

I loved Hallowe'en

because it was the only

day of the year

when I was

Beautiful

~Anna Quindlen

Dance Macabre; the mystery masquerade started in Europe in the Middle Ages, when people believed

actor in a skeleton suit,   carrying a scythe and an hour glass.

"Death,"   then disappeared

departed   from life.

or old, rich or

caped the

that the dead rose up at night to dance over their own graves.   Death was portrayed by an

People, from paupers to princes,   paraded before

as if they had   actually

No one,   young

poor,   es-

grim reaper.

Jack-O'-Lantern

PUMPKIN

AFTER ITS LID
IS CUT, THE SLICK
SEEDS AND STUCK
WET STRINGS
SCOOPED OUT,
WALLS SCRAPED
DRY AND WHITE,
FACE CARVED, CANDLE
FIXED AND LIT,

LIGHT CREEPS
INTO THE THICK
RIND: GIVING
THAT DEAD ORANGE
VEGETABLE SKULL
WARM SKIN, MAKING
A LIVE HEAD
TO HOLD ITS
SHARP GOLD GRIN.

~VALERIE WORTH

One Hallowe'en night, a
ne'er-do-well named Stingy Jack
played a trick on the Devil.
When Jack died, he was refused
entry at the gates of heaven, and
at the entrance to hell, the
Devil told him to go away,
throwing him one small glowing piece
of coal to ward off the
darkness. Jack put the ember into

I AM A JACK-O'-LANTERN WITH TERRIBLE TEETH.

-CARL SANDBURG

a hollowed-out turnip and since
then has wandered the earth
with only his jack-o'-lantern to
light his way.
—Irish Legend

27

Here are eyes and teeth and noses to trace and use to make jack-o'-lanterns from pumpkins large and small.